Highlights

W9-AUP-139

P
PRESCHOOL
AGES 3–5

Numbers
Learning Fun Workbook

For information about permission to reproduce selections from this book for an entire school or school district, please contact permissions@highlights.com.

Published by Highlights Learning • 815 Church Street • Honesdale, Pennsylvania 18431
ISBN: 978-1-68437-280-5
Mfg. 06/2020
Printed in Brainerd, MN, USA
First edition
10 9 8 7 6 5 4

For assistance in the preparation of this book, the editors would like to thank:
Vanessa Maldonado, MSEd; MS Literacy Ed. K–12; Reading/LA Consultant Cert.; K–5 Literacy Instructional Coach
Kristin Ward, MS Curriculum, Instruction, and Assessment; K–5 Mathematics Instructional Coach
Jump Start Press, Inc.

I

one

This is the number I.

This is the word **one**.

This is one way to show I.

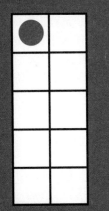

Trace the number I. Then write your own.

Find and count: I sailboat and I airplane.
What other groups of I can you find?

Answers

Page 4
2 two

Page 5
2 two

Pages 6-7
3 three

Here are some groups of 3 we found: telephone poles, trees, houses, squirrels, clouds. You might have found others.

Pages 8-9
4 four

Pages 10-11
5 five

Here are some groups of 5 we found: balloons, plates, forks, napkins, gifts, kids. You might have found others.

Pages 12-13
Count Again: 1 to 5
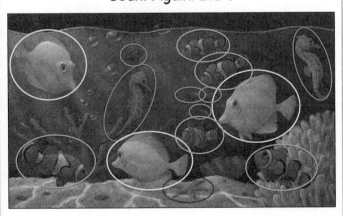

Pages 14-15
6 six

Page 17
7 seven
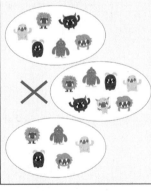

Pages 18-19
8 eight

Pages 20-21
9 nine

The dad in car number 9 is wearing a racing uniform.

Pages 24-25 Count Again: 6 to 10

Answers

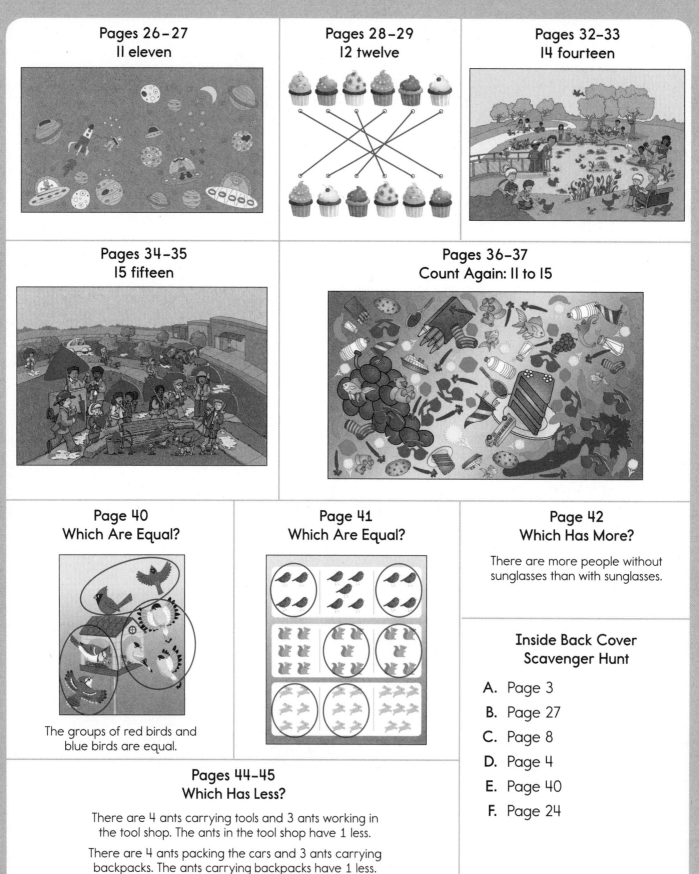

Pages 26–27
11 eleven

Pages 28–29
12 twelve

Pages 32–33
14 fourteen

Pages 34–35
15 fifteen

Pages 36–37
Count Again: 11 to 15

Page 40
Which Are Equal?

The groups of red birds and blue birds are equal.

Page 41
Which Are Equal?

Page 42
Which Has More?

There are more people without sunglasses than with sunglasses.

Inside Back Cover
Scavenger Hunt

A. Page 3

B. Page 27

C. Page 8

D. Page 4

E. Page 40

F. Page 24

Pages 44–45
Which Has Less?

There are 4 ants carrying tools and 3 ants working in the tool shop. The ants in the tool shop have 1 less.

There are 4 ants packing the cars and 3 ants carrying backpacks. The ants carrying backpacks have 1 less.

HAPPY SUMMER!

2
two

This is the number 2.

This is the word **two**.

This is one way to show 2.

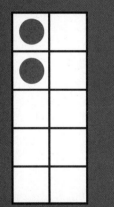

Trace the number 2. Then write your own.

2 2

Count the **2** mother cats.

Then follow the paths to help the **2** cats find their kittens.

See the black-and-white kitten peeking at you?
Find a matching kitten to make **2**.

Then find and count the other
kittens that match.

3
three

This is the number 3.

This is the word **three**.

This is one way to show 3.

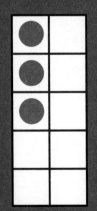

Trace the number **3**. Then write your own.

How many birds do you see?

How many benches do you see?

What other groups of **3** do you see?

4
four

Trace the number 4. Then write your own.

This is the number 4.

This is the word **four**.

This is one way to show 4.

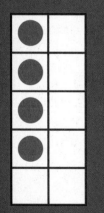

Count 4 tractors. Count 4 wagons.

Now follow each path to see which wagon each tractor will pull.

Can you name 4 foods that might grow on a farm?

9

5

five

This is the number 5.

This is the word five.

This is one way to show 5.

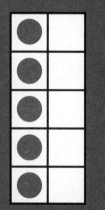

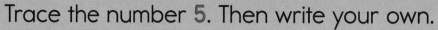

Count 5 candles on the cake.

What other groups of 5 can you find?

Count Again: 1 to 5

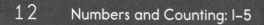

Find and count: 1 starfish, 2 seahorses, 3 yellow tang, 4 blue fish, and 5 clownfish.

6

six

This is the number 6.

This is the word six.

This is one way to show 6.

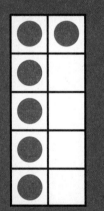

Trace the number 6. Then write your own.

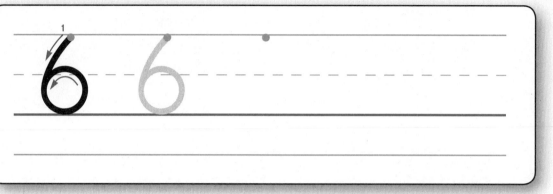

How many animals do you see in the picture on this page?

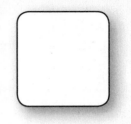

Now look at both pictures.
Find and circle **6** things that are different around the table.
Find and circle **6** things that are different in the room.

7

seven

This is the
number 7.

This is the
word **seven**.

This is
one way
to show 7.

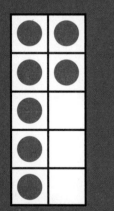

Trace the number 7. Then write your own.

Count the 7 monsters below.

Count the monsters in each group.
Put an X next to the group that has 7 monsters.
Which is your favorite monster on this page? Why?

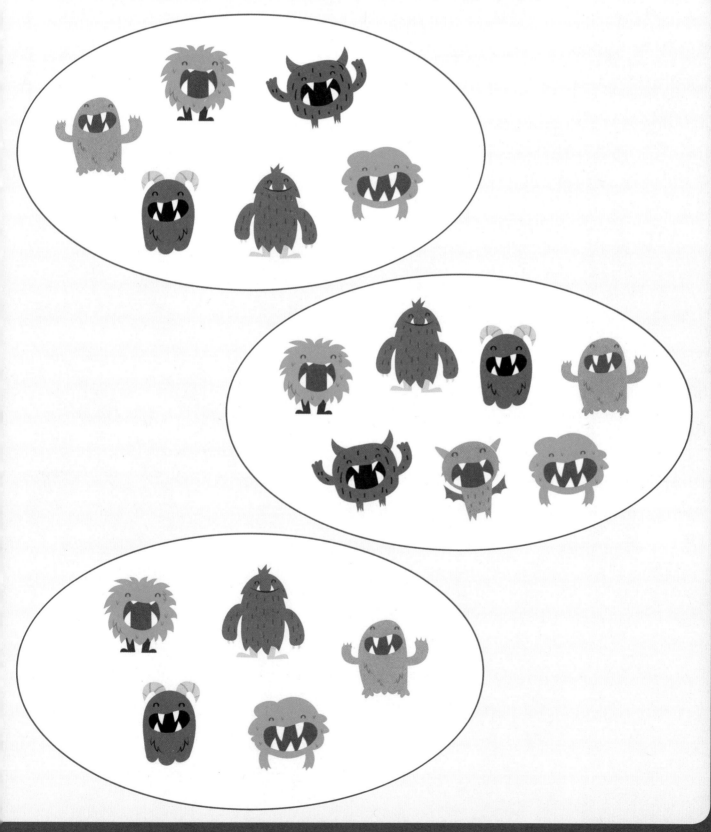

8
eight

This is the
number 8.

This is the
word **eight**.

This is
one way
to show 8.

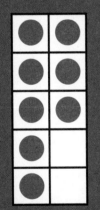

Trace the number 8. Then write your own.

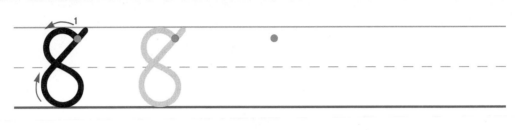

Count the 8 arms on the octopus.

How many fish can you count?

Now find 8 objects in this Hidden Pictures® puzzle.

gumdrop

binoculars

mouse

pencil

domino

snowflake

bumblebee

mop

9

nine

This is the number 9.

This is the word **nine**.

This is one way to show 9.

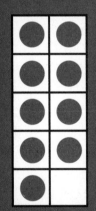

Count 9 bumper cars. What is the dad in car 9 wearing? That's silly! Look for 9 other silly things in the picture.

Can you name 2 other amusement park rides?

ten

This is the number 10.

This is the word ten.

This is one way to show 10.

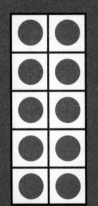

Trace the number 10. Then write your own.

Oh, no! The cat is chasing the mice. How many mice do you see?

Count and circle 10 pieces of cheese—one for each mouse!

Count Again: 6 to 10

Find and count: 6 ice-cream cones, 7 balloons, 8 pairs of sunglasses, 9 butterflies, and 10 stars. Cross off as you count.

What silly things do you see?

Be back

11

eleven

This is the number 11.

This is the word **eleven**.

This is one way to show 11.

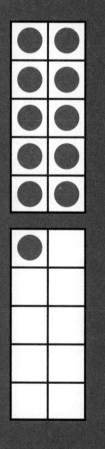

Trace the number 11. Then write your own.

acorn

binoculars

needle

paper clip

worm

slice of lemon

Count 11 planets. Then find 11 objects in this Hidden Pictures® puzzle.

fried
egg

hot dog

adhesive
bandage

football

olive

12
twelve

This is the number 12.

This is the word **twelve**.

This is one way to show 12.

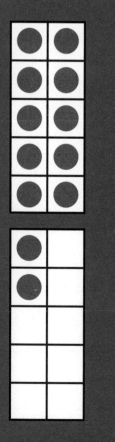

Trace the number 12. Then write your own.

Count the cupcakes on this page. How many did you count?

Draw lines to match the cupcakes that are the same.

Color the cupcakes to decorate them.

How many cupcakes did you color?

13
thirteen

This is the number 13.

This is the word thirteen.

This is one way to show 13.

Trace the number 13. Then write your own.

Would you rather be playing music or dancing? Why?

Count the 13 animals. Then color them in.

14

fourteen

This is the number 14.

This is the word fourteen.

This is one way to show 14.

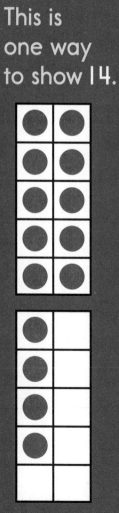

Find and count 14 ducks in the picture.
Put an X by each one as you count.

What
other
animals
do you
see?

15

fifteen

This is the number 15.

This is the word fifteen.

This is one way to show 15.

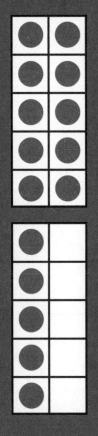

Trace the number 15. Then write your own.

Find and count **15** people.
Remember to cross off as you count.
Now find and circle **15** umbrellas.

Can you find the 2 matching umbrellas?

STOP

Flower Fill-Ins

Write the missing numbers from 1 to 5.

Write the missing numbers from 6 to 10.

Write the missing numbers from 11 to 15.

Write the missing numbers from 1 to 5.

Write the missing numbers from 6 to 10.

Write the missing numbers from 11 to 15.

Which Are Equal?

Circle each group of birds that are the same color. Count each group. Which **2** groups are equal, or have the same number?

Numbers and Counting: Equal Groups

Count the groups of each type of animal.
Circle the **2** groups that are equal in
each row.

These groups are equal. They have the same number.

Which Has More?

Find **3** open umbrellas and **1** closed umbrella. There are **more** open umbrellas. Count the people with sunglasses. Count the people without sunglasses. Which group has more?

Count each group. Then draw a group of circles that shows 1 more. We did one to get you started.

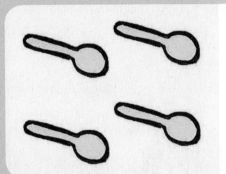

Which Has Less?

3 ants carry food. 2 ants cook. The group of ants cooking has 1 less.

Which group has 1 less:
Ants carrying tools or ants working in the tool shop?
Ants packing the cars or ants carrying backpacks?

Highlights

P PRESCHOOL

Congratulations!

_____
(your name)

worked hard
and finished the

Numbers

Learning Fun Workbook